Threads of Revelation Series

COVENANT KEEPERS:
A LEGACY FORGED

PAT DENIM

Reviews are important to independent authors, so if you have the time, I would really appreciate you leaving one for this book. Thank you.

Pat Denim

Threads of Revelation

COVENANT KEEPERS:
A Legacy Forged

Copyright © 2023 Pat Denim. All rights reserved. No part of this book may be reproduced or used in any manner without the prior written permission of the copyright owner or in accordance with the provisions of the Copyright, Designs and Patents Act 1988 or under the terms of any licence permitting limited copying issued by the Copyright Licensing Agency.

Cover Design by: Scatterling Design

Paperback: ISBN 978-1-962097-06-2
Ebook : ISBN 978-1-962097-07-9

Library of Congress Control Number: 2023946976

Table of Contents

Wandering Souls	8
Facing The Unknown	10
Scarlet Thread	12
River's Passage	14
Memory Stones	16
Captain's Wisdom	18
Seven Trumpets	20
The Accursed Thing	22
Ambush	24
Trapped By Deceit	28
Five Kings In A Cave	31
Gathering Of Kings	34
Kings In Chains	38
Unfinished Business	41
Dividing The Land	44
Inheriting Canaan	46
The Tale Of Tribes	47
Challenge Of The Forest	49
Casting The Dice	51
Tribe By Tribe	53
Fleeing Vengeance	55
Sanctuary Cities	57
The Altar	59
Time Of Reflection	61
The Covenant Stone	64
Unfinished Conquests	67
The Angel's Rebuke	70

The Strongman's Downfall	72
Cunning Deed	74
Freed From Chains	76
Impoverished Hearts	79
Torchlight Strategy	82
Troubled House	84
The Tower's Refuge	87
Idols And Enemies	90
Tragic Vow Fulfilled	92
The Jordan Crossing	96
A Fearsome Sight	98
The Betrayal	100
Fiery Retribution	102
Collapse Of The Temple	105
The Missing Silver	108
Dancing With Shadows	110
Dark Secrets	113
Endless Night	116
Sin In The Streets	118
Bitter Return	120
Hope On The Horizon	122
Midnight Encounter	125
Sealed With A Shoe	127

WANDERING SOULS

In lands where history's tapestry is spun,
Three tales revealed what was done,
In battles bold and daring flight,
A promised land, with foes to smite.

They crossed the Jordan's rushing flow,
With faith and courage, hearts aglow,
City walls fell when trumpet's sound,
Conquest complete, their victory crowned.

In cities conquered, they took their stand,
Dividing the land, a faithful band,
Yet some still clung to their idols and sin,
Leaders urged them, choose God within.

They spoke of faith, a lasting creed,
Covenants sealed, solemn deeds,
As for them and theirs, they'd obey the Lord,
In their days, their spirits soared.

Then came the time of leaders true,
Rising to guide, God's path to pursue,
But the people went so often astray,
That judges rose to light their way.

Wisdom and might, courage and light,
Strength to lead and dispel the night,
In faith they stood, both flawed and bold,
Their stories told, the ages unfold.

In foreign lands, love's sweet refrain,
A tale of faith, parting to much pain,
A journey begun, a virtuous plan,
Kindness entwined, by God's own hand.

In fields of toil, a humble start,
A gleaner's path, where love did chart,
A man's kindness, two lives entwine,
A timeless story, blessed, divine.

These tales of old, their stories told,
Of battles, faith, and love, extolled,
Of courage, grace, and sacred lore,
In these stories, we find much more.

FACING THE UNKNOWN

In days now past, Moses passed away,
The Lord to Joshua had this to say,
"Arise, O Joshua, my servant dear,
Lead the people and do not fear.

Moses is gone, a new chapter begins,
Cross Jordan's flow, where hope begins.
From wilderness to Euphrates' shore,
The land I promise is yours to explore.

No one shall stand against your might,
As I was with Moses day and night.
Be strong and brave, let courage grow,
Inherit the land where your children will go.

Follow the law, stay on the track,
Turn not aside, and never look back.
Keep it close, day and night to heed,
Prosperity and success shall you feed.

Don't be afraid, in your stride,
I am with you, your faithful guide.
Joshua, my command, do not ignore,
For I am with you forevermore.

To the officers Joshua then said,
Prepare yourselves, be well-fed.
Three days' time, Jordan you'll span,
Into the promised land, God's own plan.

For Reubenites, Gadites, Manasseh's kin,
Remember the words that did begin,
Moses' promise of rest and land anew,
Stand as mighty valiant, steadfast and true.

When brethren find rest, the land they claim,
Then to your homes you'll happily aim.
With hearts full of faith and promises grand,
Obey Joshua's lead in this blessed land.

With one voice, they pledged their vow,
To Joshua they said, "We'll follow you now.
As we heeded Moses in days of yore,
May God's presence with you evermore.

Those who rebel shall meet their fate,
Death awaits those who deviate.
Be strong, be brave, with courage thrive,
With God's guidance and grace, we will survive."

PAT DENIM

SCARLET THREAD

From Shittim's camp, two spies did go,
Secretly to Jericho, they'd show,
"Explore the land," Joshua declared,
Jericho's secrets they would not spare.

To Rahab's house, the men did roam,
A harlot's dwelling, far from home,
The king of Jericho soon was told,
Israel's scouts were brave and bold.

The king commanded, Rahab, bring forth,
The men who came from distant North,
To spy on us, our land explore,
But Rahab's heart held something more.

She hid the men upon her roof,
With stalks of flax, a clever spoof,
As dark set in and gate shut tight,
The spies departed into the night.

To Jordan's fords, they made their way,
Pursuers followed, night and day,
But Rahab helped them slip away,
A cord let them descend and sway.

"I know the Lord has favored you,
Fear grips our hearts, our courage through,
The Red Sea's parting, tales we've heard,
Of Amorite kings, your mighty word.

Our hearts did melt, no courage remains,
The Lord your God in heaven reigns,
I beg you now, in kindness sworn,
Protect my kin, when land is torn."

The spies agreed, a pact was made,
Kindness for kindness, debt repaid,
Through window's frame, a scarlet thread,
A sign of safety, life to spread.

To the mountain's sanctuary they fled,
Three days they hid, no foe ahead,
Back to Joshua they would later tell,
How Rahab's kindness weaved its spell.

"We found the land as you had said,
The people's hearts are filled with dread,
The LORD has given it to our hand,
Jericho's fate, as He had planned."

And so the tale of spies and thread,
How Rahab helped, her courage spread,
In Jericho's city, a shining star,
A part in Israel's journey far.

RIVER'S PASSAGE

When morning sun lit up the skies,
From Shittim's grounds, they did arise.
Joshua and Israel, by Jordan's shore,
A journey new, a destiny in store.

Three days passed, officers took lead,
Through the host they went with heed.
"When the ark of the LORD you see,
Follow it on, and so it shall be,

Keep some distance, a measured space,
Two thousand cubits to keep the pace.
This sacred vessel, this holy guide,
Will show you the way, no need to hide.

Sanctify yourselves," Joshua did proclaim,
"For wondrous deeds the Lord will frame.
Priests, lift the ark, lead the way ahead,
With faith in our hearts, let's move ahead."

To the priests, the Lord did declare,
In Joshua's rise, His presence to bear,
"I'll magnify you in Israel's sight,
As I did with Moses, day and night."

At Jordan's brink, priests stood still,
Joshua spoke, with a divine will,
"Come, children of Israel, lend an ear,
Hear the words of God, clear and near.

Know that the living God is here,
He'll drive your foes, do not fear.
Canaanites, Hittites, and tribes so vast,
Before His might, they will not last."

The ark of the covenant, a sign so true,
Passing before them, water's blue.
Twelve men, one from each tribe's array,
Step forth, their journey to convey.

As priests' feet touch Jordan's stream,
Waters part like a wondrous dream.
They stand on dry ground, the river's tide,
In awe, the people watch and bide.

Water rose, a wall so high,
A passage opened, without a sigh.
The Israelites marched, their hearts ablaze,
Through parted waters, a path they raise.

Priests and ark stood firm and sound,
On dry ground, they were firmly bound.
All the people crossed over too,
Jordan's miracle, God's promise true.

MEMORY STONES

When Jordan's waters they did cross,
The Lord to Joshua then did toss,
"Choose twelve men, each tribe shall bring,
From midst of Jordan, take a thing.

Twelve stones, these men shall carry hence,
A sign, a tale of providence.
Where you lodge tonight, they shall lay,
A memorial to guide your way."

So Joshua called, each tribe's own man,
Prepared them well, as God's own plan.
"Pass before the ark," Joshua decreed,
"Take a stone each, as you proceed.

For your children's queries in days ahead,
These stones shall speak, when they are led,
To ask of the meaning, the purpose here,
Of these stones that memory holds dear.

Tell them the waters were held at bay,
By the ark of the Lord that passed this way.
A reminder eternal, a story to tell,
How Jordan's waters, like a wall, did swell."

As commanded, Israel did comply,
From Jordan's midst, the stones did fly.
Joshua set them up in that very place,
Where priests had stood in God's embrace.

Priests bore the ark, its sacred weight,
In Jordan's midst, they did await.
When they emerged, and land was dry,
Jordan's flow returned, waves reaching high.

On the tenth day of the first month's light,
Israel stood at Gilgal's site.
Twelve stones from Jordan, Joshua did lay,
A witness to God's mighty display.

And Joshua spoke, a charge to bear,
For generations yet to share,
"When children ask, these stones to see,
Tell them how God led you free.

Through parted waters, dry ground trod,
Just as He did for Moses, God,
Dried the Red Sea, and now the Jordan,
So all may know His power unbroken.

That the people of the earth might stand,
In awe of God's mighty hand.
Fear the Lord, the One above,
His strength, His grace, His boundless love."

CAPTAIN'S WISDOM

When Amorite and Canaanite kings,
Heard of Jordan's miraculous things,
Their hearts grew weak, their spirits fell,
Before the might that Israel could quell.

At that time, to Joshua came the word,
A second circumcision, a rite to be heard.
"Make sharp knives," the Lord did say,
Circumcise the children without delay.

Sharp knives Joshua did prepare,
Upon the hill, the ritual to bear,
For all who'd come from Egypt's land,
The men of war, a faithful band.

In the wilderness, for forty years they roamed,
Men of war perished, as they had been forewarned,
Those born along the desert way,
Had not received the mark that day.

For they did not heed the Lord's command,
In the wilderness, they could not stand.
But their children, now in their stead,
Joshua circumcised, as God had said.

When all were circumcised, they stayed,
In the camp, their wounds to fade.
The Lord declared, "Egypt's shame is done,
The place is Gilgal, victory is won."

In Gilgal, they encamped with grace,
Celebrated Passover in that place,
Ate unleavened cakes of old,
And parched corn, a tale to be told.

Manna ceased as the land they trod,
They ate the fruits, the blessings of God.
By Jericho, Joshua stood in awe,
A man with drawn sword, a sight to draw.

"Are you friend or foe?" Joshua asked,
"Neither," he replied, his voice steadfast,
"I'm captain of the host of the Lord,
In holy presence, you stand restored."

Joshua fell, his face to the ground,
Worshipping the captain he had found,
"Speak, my lord," Joshua inquired,
The captain's wisdom, he desired.

"Take off your shoes," the captain decreed,
"For where you stand is holy indeed."
Joshua obeyed, on sacred land,
A divine encounter, God's mighty hand.

SEVEN TRUMPETS

Jericho's gates were tightly sealed,
No one entered, none revealed.
The Lord said, "Jericho is yours,
With its king and valiant force."

Six days around the city go,
Seven priests with trumpets blow.
On the seventh day, march around,
Seven times, the walls unbound.

With a long blast, a mighty shout,
The walls crumbled, there was no doubt.
The city laid bare, the people climbed,
Obedience and faith combined.

But the city was set aside,
A curse upon it, they were advised.
Rahab alone, the harlot, saved,
For her kindness, her life paved.

No silver, gold, or iron kept,
All consecrated, the Lord's treasure swept.
With a mighty shout, the walls fell down,
Victory was claimed by Israel's renown.

They destroyed all, man and beast,
City's fate was thus released.
To Rahab's house the spies did fare,
Rescued her and her kin with care.

Jericho burnt by fire's breath,
Only treasure for the Lord's house, no death.
Rahab and kin found their place,
In Israel, a new life's embrace.

Joshua declared a solemn vow,
Cursed the rebuilder of Jericho's brow.
With the Lord by Joshua's side,
His fame spread far and wide.

THE ACCURSED THING

The children of Israel sinned indeed,
Achan's transgression caused them to bleed.
He took the accursed, against God's command,
And the Lord's anger swept the land.

Joshua sent men to Ai's abode,
To scout the country, a plan he showed.
Two or three thousand men he chose,
To smite Ai's few, his strategy goes.

They fled in fear before Ai's might,
Thirty-six fell in the desperate fight.
Hearts like water, courage drained,
Joshua grieved, his spirit pained.

With clothes rent and dust on his head,
Before the Lord, Joshua knelt and pled,
"Why lead us here, just to be lost?
Give us strength to face the cost."

The Lord replied, "Get up, arise,
Israel sinned, a grave compromise.
An accursed thing within you lies,
Remove it now, heed my advice."

The people were sanctified, prepared,
The accursed thing they must be spared.
Tribe by tribe, man by man,
The guilty would be known, God's plan.

Judah's tribe, then Zerah's line,
Achan's name came forth, a dark sign.
"My son," said Joshua, "confess your sin,
Tell me all, let the truth begin."

Achan admitted with heavy heart,
He coveted and took, his greed a part.
Babylonish garment, silver, gold,
In his tent's depths, his secret bold.

Messengers ran to unveil the sin,
Achan's loot hidden deep within.
Before the Lord, the treasures laid,
Achan's guilt could not evade.

With heavy hearts and solemn pace,
Joshua and Israel moved to erase,
The sin's foul stain, the Lord's command,
They stoned and burned upon the land.

A heap of stones marked the place so grim,
The valley of Achor, a name for him.
The Lord's anger turned, fierce no more,
The price of sin, they bore and bore.

AMBUSH

The Lord spoke to Joshua, "Do not fear,
Take your warriors and draw near,
To Ai you shall go, victory is sure,
I'll deliver the king, his people, and more."

Like Jericho, you shall do,
Conquer the city, the king too,
Only the spoils and cattle shall be,
A reward for your victory, you'll see.

Joshua selected valiant men,
Thirty thousand, a chosen ken,
He sent them to lie in wait at night,
An ambush hidden, out of sight.

"Draw them out, then flee as before,
They'll follow, thinking you implore,
The city is yours, rise from the ploy,
For the Lord shall your efforts deploy."

Joshua numbered his men in sight,
Elders with him, preparing for the fight,
They approached Ai, pitched by its wall,
A valley between them, where they would fall.

Five thousand more laid in wait nearby,
On the west side, hidden from the eye,
The ambush was set, the plan prepared,
Joshua waited, his heart declared.

When Ai's king saw and his men arose,
To battle they went, thinking to oppose,
But in the ambush, they knew not of,
Their doom awaited, their fate to prove.

Joshua's men feigned a flight in haste,
Ai pursued, their victory chased,
The city they left, unguarded behind,
Their foolishness hidden, a plan aligned.

Then Joshua stretched his spear in hand,
The Lord declared, His command,
The ambush arose, they stormed the town,
Fire engulfed it, the walls came down.

Ai's men turned, saw the city's doom,
Smoke rose high, sealing their tomb,
They fled to the wilderness in fright,
Only to meet the pursuing might.

Joshua and Israel saw their chance,
With ambush and warriors in a dance,
They conquered Ai, a fierce attack,
None were left, none turned back.

The king of Ai, now captured, brought,
To Joshua's feet, his reign was naught,
All the inhabitants met their fate,
In the wilderness, their story would abate.

Twelve thousand men and women fell,
By the edge of the sword, they'd quell,
Joshua's hand held the spear steady,
Until the city's end was ready.

Only cattle and spoils they'd keep,
As the Lord's command they'd steep,
The city of Ai, consumed by flame,
Forever a heap, bearing its name.

The king of Ai hung on a tree,
A solemn reminder for all to see,
Joshua's obedience to the Lord's word,
A lesson of justice, clearly heard.

At Mount Ebal, an altar rose,
Built as Moses' law bestows,
Offerings and sacrifices made,
God's covenant, firmly laid.

Upon the stones, the law was writ,
A testimony to never forget,
The people, the elders, and leaders too,
Blessings and curses, before them grew.

Joshua read the words of old,
Moses' commands, stories told,
Before the congregation, women and men,
Strangers and natives, a diverse blend.

Not a word of Moses' law did he miss,
Read before them, nothing amiss,
The people gathered, a solemn crowd,
In God's covenant, they were endowed.

TRAPPED BY DECEIT

When the kings beyond Jordan's shore,
Hittite, Amorite, Jebusite and more,
Heard of the victories Joshua had won,
They united their forces as one.

Gibeon, a city near,
Heard of Jericho and Ai in fear,
They devised a cunning plan,
To save themselves from Israel's hand.

They dressed in worn clothes and shoes,
With old sacks, dry bread to use,
As ambassadors, they'd appear,
Seeking peace and partnership sincere.

To Joshua's camp at Gilgal they went,
Claiming to be from a distant land sent,
"Make a league with us," they beseeched,
Hoping their lies would not be reached.

Israel questioned their intent,
"Are you our neighbors, truly sent?"
Gibeon replied with a fabricated tale,
Claiming distance and a journey frail.

They said, "Our elders advised us so,
To make a league with you and go,
Our bread was hot when we left our home,
Now it's dry and moldy, we do bemoan."

Bottles of wine they displayed,
Claiming they were new, not decayed,
Their garments and shoes were old and worn,
From a journey long, they had borne.

Israel took their provisions, trusting not,
They sought no counsel from the Lord's thought,
Joshua made peace, a league was sealed,
Princes swore an oath, the truth concealed.

Three days passed and the truth came clear,
Gibeon dwelled close, their ruse severe,
The cities were theirs, not from afar,
A deception, a lie, like a fallen star.

Israel murmured at the princes' choice,
Sworn by the Lord, they voiced their voice,
"We've made an oath," the princes said,
To harm them now would make us dread.

Hewers of wood and water drawers they'd be,
A promise to serve for eternity,
Gibeon's trickery had them ensnared,
Bound to servitude, as the princes declared.

Joshua confronted them in ire,
"Why deceive us with such attire?
You live among us, it is clear,
Now servitude for you is near."

Gibeon confessed their plan laid bare,
Afraid of their fate, they chose to share,
Moses' command to conquer all,
Had filled them with fear, their voices small.

They placed themselves in Israel's hand,
Accepting any fate that would stand,
Joshua spared their lives that day,
But servitude they couldn't sway.

They became hewers of wood and more,
Drawers of water, a life to endure,
For Israel's altar, for God's abode,
In service they found their unchanging road.

FIVE KINGS IN A CAVE

Adonizedek, Jerusalem's king bold,
Heard of Ai's fall and Gibeon's fold,
Feared greatly Gibeon's might and size,
With its royal city's enterprise.

He summoned other kings of the land,
Hoham, Piram, Japhia took a stand,
Together, they sought to smite Gibeon's head,
For it with Israel had peace instead.

The kings of the Amorites arose,
Jerusalem, Hebron, Lachish in rows,
They encamped around Gibeon's walls,
War's trumpet sounded, destiny calls.

Gibeon sent for Joshua to aid,
"Come save us, don't let our fate be laid,
The Amorite kings have gathered might,
Help us now, before endless night."

Joshua and his warriors stood,
Fierce and ready for battle's blood,
The Lord assured, "Fear not, be bold,
I've delivered them into your hold."

Joshua marched from Gilgal's site,
Through the night, his heart alight,
The LORD struck the enemy down,
With Gibeon's defenders, a united crown.

From Gibeon's field to Bethhoron's way,
The enemy fled, in disarray,
Hailstones rained down, their end was near,
More died from above than by sword's spear.

In that day's midst, Joshua did pray,
"Sun, stand still," the night to delay,
And the moon halted in Ajalon's vale,
As Israel avenged, their foes to assail.

A day like that had never been,
When God heeded a man's voice unseen,
The Lord fought fiercely, His power shown,
For Israel, victory brightly shone.

Joshua and his forces returned in peace,
To Gilgal's camp, where troubles cease,
Five kings in a cave were found,
Joshua commanded, stones to mound.

He pursued the fleeing enemies strong,
Allowed none to their cities throng,
Fenced cities sheltered the remaining,
Israel's victory was truly gaining.

Five kings were brought forth from the cave's night,
Their necks under Israel's warriors' might,
Joshua declared, "Fear not, take heart,
God delivers your enemies to depart."

The kings were slain and hanged on trees,
A testimony of God's decrees,
At sunset's hour, their bodies fell,
Into the cave where they tried to dwell.

Joshua conquered cities, one by one,
Makkedah, Libnah, battles won,
Lachish and Eglon, cities they took,
The Amorites' strength they forsook.

Hebron, Debir, and more in line,
Conquered by Israel's might divine,
Joshua obeyed the Lord's command,
No enemy stood by His hand.

Joshua's conquest covered hill and vale,
From Kadeshbarnea to Gibeon's tale,
The Lord fought for Israel with grace,
Victory seen in each war's embrace.

And so, Joshua and Israel returned,
To Gilgal's camp, where courage burned,
God's hand was shown through their campaign,
His power and might, their victory's gain.

PAT DENIM

GATHERING OF KINGS

Jabin, Hazor's king, took alarm,
Sent to kings to raise a storm,
Jobab of Madon, Shimron's king,
Achshaph's ruler, their forces bring.

Kings from north and south arise,
From Chinneroth's plains to distant skies,
Canaanite, Amorite, many a name,
Gathered together, their might to claim.

Hivite, Hittite, Jebusite strong,
Perizzite, too, their forces throng,
As the sand on the shore, countless and vast,
With horses and chariots, their armies amassed.

At Merom's waters, they converged,
Against Israel's might, they surged,
But the Lord spoke to Joshua, clear,
"Fear not, victory is near."

On the morrow, they would fall,
Defeated by God's sovereign call,
Their horses houghed, their chariots burned,
Israel's triumph firmly earned.

Joshua and his warriors bold,
By Merom's waters, they were told,
To strike the enemy, without delay,
And thus, the battle's course did sway.

Israel prevailed, their foes were chased,
To Zidon's great shores, they raced,
Misrephothmaim, the valley's name,
Eastern Mizpeh, they met their shame.

As commanded by God's own voice,
Joshua followed, made the choice,
Houghed the horses, chariots aflame,
Executing the Lord's righteous claim.

Returning victorious, Joshua's might,
He conquered Hazor in the fight,
Once the head of these domains,
Now fallen by Israel's pains.

All the souls in Hazor's keep,
By sword's edge, they fell deep,
The city razed by fire's breath,
Hazor's empire met its death.

All those kings and their domains,
Joshua conquered, broke their chains,
All perished by the sword's stroke,
Moses' command, to them bespoke.

Yet cities standing strong and firm,
From their fire, Israel did affirm,
Except Hazor, burned in fire's embrace,
The rest preserved by mercy's grace.

Spoils and cattle, Israel gained,
Their enemies' strength was strained,
But every warrior, by sword's grace,
Was defeated, left no trace.

Joshua followed God's command,
As Moses spoke in the Promised Land,
Taking the hills, the valleys wide,
Goshen's expanse, in God's stride.

From Halak's mount to Lebanon's vale,
Joshua's might did never fail,
Seir to Baalgad, mountains and plain,
All the kings conquered, victory's gain.

Anakims too, giants of old,
Joshua defeated, the tale is told,
From Hebron, Debir, mountains grand,
Israel's conquest swept the land.

Anakims lingered in Gaza's hold,
In Gath, Ashdod, stories unfold,
But Joshua prevailed, the whole land he took,
As the Lord had spoken, in every nook.

The land was settled, tribes divided,
By Joshua's rule, as God decided,
War's tumult ceased, its fury ceased,
The land lay quiet, in God's peace.

KINGS IN CHAINS

Kings of the land, their fate is told,
Israel's conquest, a story bold,
From Arnon's river, eastward sun's embrace,
To mount Hermon's peak, all they did face.

Sihon, king of the Amorite race,
In Heshbon's dwelling, held his place,
From Aroer's bank, Arnon's shore,
Ruled o'er Gilead's half, the boundary bore.

From plains to Chinneroth's eastern shore,
To salt sea's expanse, they journeyed more,
Towards Bethjeshimoth, path they trod,
Under Ashdothpisgah, southward's nod.

Og, king of Bashan, giant strong,
Ashtaroth, Edrei, his reign along,
Mount Hermon's heights, Salcah's land,
Borders of Geshurites, a vast expanse.

In Moses' time, they faced their fate,
He and Israel, determined state,
They smote the giants, claimed their own,
For Reuben, Gad, Manasseh, it was known.

West of Jordan, Joshua's might,
Kings were conquered, put to flight,
From Baalgad's vale, Lebanon's embrace,
Mount Halak's slope, to Seir's grace.

In mountains, valleys, plains so wide,
In springs, wilderness, south's pride,
Hittites, Amorites, Canaanite's sway,
Perizzites, Hivites, Jebusites' array.

Jericho's king, Ai's ruler bold,
Jerusalem's monarch, stories told,
Hebron's king, Jarmuth's might,
Lachish's ruler, in battle's light.

Eglon, Gezer, Debir's name,
Geder, Hormah, with royal claim,
Arad, Libnah, Adullam's might,
Makkedah's king, Bethel's sight.

Tappuah, Hepher, Aphek's reign,
Lasharon's king, Madon's domain,
Hazor's ruler, Shimronmeron's fame,
Achshaph's king, with known name.

Taanach, Megiddo, their power's sway,
Kedesh, Jokneam of Carmel's day,
Dor's ruler, Gilgal's might,
Tirzah's king, in battle's fight.

Kings numbered thirty-one in all,
Before Israel's might, they did fall,
Their lands conquered, tribes received,
Divided as God's plan perceived.

Unfinished Business

Joshua, old and frail in years,
The Lord's voice in his ears,
"Much land remains yet to be possessed,
A task ahead, put to the test."

Philistines' borders, Geshurites' land,
From Sihor to Ekron, all was planned,
Five lords of Philistines, their might,
Gazathites, Ashdothites in the light.

Avites, Eshkalonites, Gittites too,
Ekronites' power, among the few,
From south to Mearah, Sidon's side,
Aphek's borders, Amorite's pride.

Giblites' land, Lebanon's grace,
Mount Hermon's realm, a distant place,
Inhabitants, from Lebanon to sea,
I will drive out, make them flee.

Divide by lot, for Israel's kin,
Inheritance, a prize to win,
Nine tribes and Manasseh's half,
Reubenites, Gadites, their epitaph.

Moses gave beyond Jordan's stream,
Inheritances, like a dream,
Cities, plains, and mountain's might,
Promised lands, a shining light.

Reuben's coast by Arnon's shore,
Medeba's plain, land to explore,
Cities like Jahazah and more,
Dibon, Bamothbaal, by river's roar.

Mount of the valley, Zarethshahar's height,
Bethpeor, Ashdothpisgah's sight,
Sihon's realm, cities of plain,
Moses' conquest, victory's gain.

Balaam too, among the slain,
By Israel's sword, his end came,
Border of Reuben, Jordan's line,
Their inheritance, their claim divine.

Gad's inheritance, a tale to tell,
From Jazer's hold to Rabbah's swell,
Heshbon to Debir, land they possess,
Cities, towns, their rightful address.

Half of Manasseh, Machir's line,
From Mahanaim to cities fine,
Og's kingdom, Gilead's might,
Jair's legacy, cities of light.

Moses' work, the land they gain,
In Moab's plains, inheritance's chain,
Tribe of Levi, unique in their stand,
The Lord God of Israel, their promised land.

DIVIDING THE LAND

The land of Canaan, inheritance received,
By Eleazar and Joshua, leaders believed,
Heads of tribes, as commanded of old,
Divided the land, a story untold.

By lot it was done, as the Lord decreed,
For nine tribes and a half, a sacred seed,
Two and a half beyond Jordan's shore,
Moses' command, inheritance they bore.

Levites, no portion of land they gain,
Cities and suburbs, their dwelling's domain,
Joseph's children, Manasseh and Ephraim true,
No part for Levites, a different view.

As commanded, Israel's people obey,
Dividing the land in the light of the day,
Judah's children came, to Joshua spoke,
Caleb the Kenezite, faith never broke.

At Kadeshbarnea, Moses' decree,
Sent to explore, the land to see,
Forty years past, yet strong and bold,
God's promise fulfilled, his story told.

Brethren brought fear, but God he embraced,
His heart stayed true, not a moment erased,
Moses then swore, by His holy name,
Caleb's inheritance, forever the same.

Alive he stands, forty-five years passed by,
In wilderness wanderings, 'neath the sky,
At eighty-five, his strength remains,
For war he's prepared, as history gains.

"Give me this mountain," Caleb requests,
Anakims' land, though fenced and stressed,
Joshua blessed him, his faith to uphold,
Hebron he gained, with stories untold.

Once Kirjatharba, now Hebron's name,
Caleb's inheritance, God's eternal flame,
Rest from the war, the land to reclaim,
God's promise fulfilled, in history's frame.

INHERITING CANAAN

The tribe of Judah, with lands to gain,
The inheritance received, a territory's domain,
Southward they stretched, to Edom's reach,
Zin's wilderness, their boundary's teach.

From the salt sea's shore, they marked the line,
To Maalehacrabbim, their bounds define,
To Kadeshbarnea, they journeyed on,
From Adar to Karkaa, their path was drawn.

To Egypt's river, the border then goes,
Eastward to Jordan, where its flow shows,
Bethhogla, Debir, and more to be,
Toward Jerusalem's land, the line they see.

Jerusalem's Jebusites, they could not rout,
Among Judah's people, they remained, no doubt,
Cities and villages, a list so grand,
Caleb's inheritance, at God's command.

Such is the tale of Judah's land's spread,
Cities and borders, the tale that's read,
In the mountains, valleys, the plains so wide,
Judah's portion, by families' side.

THE TALE OF TRIBES

From Jordan's bank by Jericho they begin,
To the waters of Jericho, flowing eastward in,
Through the wilderness, up to Bethel's height,
A journey of boundaries, a land to invite.

From Bethel to Luz, Archi's borders in sight,
To Ataroth, the path leads to the light,
Westward to Japhleti, Bethhoron's nether land,
To Gezer's coast, where sea meets sand.

Manasseh and Ephraim, Joseph's kin,
Their inheritance claimed, a new chapter to begin,
Ephraim's border, on the east it lies,
From Atarothaddar to Bethhoron's rise.

Towards Michmethah, its course does unfold,
Northward to Taanathshiloh, a story of old,
To Janohah it turns, then to Ataroth's ground,
Naarath, Jericho, Jordan's flow is found.

Tappuah to the river Kanah, the border westward strides,
At the sea's edge, the journey abides,
Ephraim's inheritance, by families, defined,
A land of their own, in history enshrined.

Among Manasseh's land, Ephraim's cities found,
Side by side, their existence is bound,
Gezer's Canaanites, a challenge they face,
Among Ephraimites, in a different space.

Yet Canaanites remain, their tribute they bear,
Ephraim's story continues, a legacy to share,
Inheritance and challenge, history intertwined,
The tribes of Joseph, their destiny defined.

CHALLENGE OF THE FOREST

The tribe of Manasseh, firstborn of Joseph's line,
Received their lot, a destiny divine,
Machir, the warrior, Gilead's father bold,
With Gilead and Bashan, their inheritance unfold.

Manasseh's families, diverse and wide,
Abiezer, Helek, Asriel side by side,
Shechem, Hepher, Shemida, their names unfold,
Sons of Manasseh's lineage, stories untold.

Zelophehad's daughters, no sons to their name,
Mahlah, Noah, Hoglah, Milcah, Tirzah in fame,
Before Joshua and Eleazar, they came forth to plead,
For an inheritance, as the Lord's word decreed.

Ten portions fell to Manasseh's hand,
But Gilead and Bashan, beyond Jordan's strand,
Daughters of Manasseh claimed their rightful share,
Inheritance among sons, a testament fair.

From Asher to Michmethah, Manasseh's land spread,
Entappuah's inhabitants marked the border ahead,
Tappuah, a city, yet part of Ephraim's domain,
Unity of tribes, their boundaries to explain.

The river Kanah marked the southern line,
Ephraim and Manasseh's land intertwined,
Ephraim's land met the sea's foaming tide,
Manasseh, to Asher and Issachar's side.

Bethshean, Ibleam, and Dor, names of old,
Endor, Taanach, Megiddo's stories told,
Inhabitants remained, Canaanites stood firm,
Driving them out, a challenge to confirm.

Stronger grew Israel, their strength on display,
Canaanites subdued, yet in their midst they stay,
The children of Joseph approached with concern,
One portion, they felt, was not enough to discern.

Joshua's response echoed with wisdom and grace,
Expand to the wood country, seek a larger space,
In Perizzites' land and where giants reside,
Mount Ephraim too narrow, let your borders widen wide.

But Joseph's children voiced another plea,
The hill's not sufficient, Canaanites have chariots free,
Joshua addressed Ephraim and Manasseh with care,
Great and powerful tribe, more land they'd share.

The mountain, a forest, a challenge they'd face,
Cutting it down, they'd establish their place,
Driving out Canaanites with iron chariots strong,
Ephraim and Manasseh, they'd prove their might all along.

CASTING THE DICE

The congregation gathered at Shiloh's site,
Setting up the tabernacle, a holy rite,
The land subdued before them lay,
Yet seven tribes still sought their way.

Joshua addressed the tribes with care,
"Why delay possession, land so fair,
The Lord your fathers' God did bestow,
Rise, inherit the land you know."

Three men from each tribe, to describe the land,
Joshua commanded, a diligent band,
Dividing it into seven parts so clear,
To cast lots before the Lord, without fear.

Judah to the south, Joseph's house to the north,
The Levites, priests, held a separate worth,
Gad, Reuben, and half of Manasseh's kin,
Received their inheritance beyond Jordan's din.

Men described the land, a book was filled,
Seven parts divided, their purpose fulfilled,
Joshua cast lots before the Lord's gaze,
Dividing the land to the tribes' praise.

Benjamin's lot emerged, boundaries decreed,
Between Judah and Joseph, their portion agreed,
From Jordan's side, a border drew,
Westward through mountains, landscapes anew.

From Luz to Bethel, a southern flow,
To Atarothadar and Bethhoron below,
The southern sea corner was traced with care,
Kirjathbaal's mark in the west, beyond compare.

Southward, to Nephtoah's well it descended,
Through Hinnom's valley, the path extended,
To Enrogel, Jebusi's side it passed,
To the stone of Bohan, the border was cast.

Northward to Arabah, it traveled its way,
Passing Bethhoglah, the north bay it'd sway,
Jordan the eastern border, clear and grand,
Benjamin's inheritance, a promised land.

Cities of Benjamin, a list to share,
Jericho, Bethel, and more were there,
Gibeon, Ramah, and many more,
Twelve cities stood, their history to store.

Gibeath, Jerusalem, a city renowned,
Benjamin's inheritance, by families' bounds,
Fourteen cities strong, with villages near,
Their heritage established, their legacy clear.

TRIBE BY TRIBE

Simeon's lot, the second in line,
Within Judah's inheritance, it did shine,
Cities and villages, thirteen in sum,
Their heritage granted by God's wisdom.

Zebulun's third lot, the border's trace,
Sarid to Jordan's embrace,
Cities twelve with villages by the coast,
Their inheritance defined, no detail lost.

Fourthly, Issachar's lot was shown,
Jezreel, Chesulloth, cities well-known,
Sixteen cities with their domains,
Their inheritance by their families' claims.

Asher's tribe, fifth in the queue,
Received their portion, a land anew,
Twenty-two cities strong and sure,
Their inheritance clear, to endure.

Sixthly, Naphtali, with borders wide,
Cities and villages to provide,
Nineteen cities with their claim,
Their inheritance, their ancient name.

Seventh, Dan's tribe, took their place,
Cities with strength, their space to grace,
Cities and their villages, they gained,
An inheritance defined, their destiny ordained.

When the land's division was complete,
Joshua, by the Lord's word to meet,
Received a city, a reward so just,
In Ephraim's mount, a place to trust.

Eleazar the priest and Joshua, too,
Heads of tribes, their work they knew,
By lot in Shiloh, God's guidance true,
Divided the land, the nation grew.

FLEEING VENGEANCE

The Lord to Joshua then did say,
"Appoint cities of refuge, I convey,
As I spoke by Moses, you must heed,
Those who've caused another's death unheed."

A place of refuge for those who slew,
Unwittingly, without hatred, too,
From the avenger of blood they'd flee,
A shelter for all, a sanctuary.

At the city gate, the fleeing stands,
Declares his case to the city's hands,
The elders hear, and provide a space,
Where he may dwell, in this safe place.

If the avenger pursues with might,
They shall not yield him to their fight,
For he struck unknowing, without ill will,
A refuge granted, his blood to still.

In the city he dwells till judgment's near,
Before the congregation he must appear,
Till the high priest's death, his time is spent,
Then he returns, to his own intent.

Kedesh in Galilee, Shechem, too,
Hebron's Kirjatharba, for refuge they drew,
On Jordan's east side, cities of grace,
Bezer, Ramoth, Golan's embrace.

For all of Israel, and the stranger as well,
These cities provided, where they could dwell,
A place to escape the avenger's quest,
Until before the congregation they're addressed.

SANCTUARY CITIES

The Levite fathers came to stand,
Before Eleazar, Joshua's hand,
In Shiloh's land, where they did say,
"The Lord's command we must obey."

Cities of refuge, they request,
With suburbs wide, where cattle rest,
Israel complied, gave them their due,
For Levites' side, these cities grew.

For Kohath's line, by Judah's side,
Thirteen they find, their homes to bide,
From Simeon and Benjamin,
Their lots assigned, cities within.

Ephraim and Dan, tribes they did glean,
For Kohath's clan, ten cities seen,
Gershon then found, their portion near,
From Issachar's ground, and Asher's sphere.

Merari took their cities, too,
From Reuben's nook, and Zebulun true,
Gad's land was shared, as was decreed,
Levites prepared, their homes to lead.

The Levites' share was all in all,
Cities to spare, at God's own call,
Families known, to them were given,
Cities of stone, by lot from heaven.

Cities of refuge, sanctuary,
For those accused, a place to be,
Levites' abode, within these bounds,
Forty-eight bestowed, peace resounds.

God's promise grand, now fulfilled,
In every land, their foes were stilled,
Rest from their toil, as sworn of old,
On victory's soil, their story told.

Not a word misplaced, nor plan awry,
All God's promise embraced, under the sky,
Israel's fortune amassed, a faithful hand,
Their future held fast, by God's command.

THE ALTAR

To Reuben, Gad, and Manasseh's part,
Joshua spoke, his words from heart,
"You've followed well the Lord's command,
Obeyed my voice throughout the land.

You've not abandoned brethren true,
All through these days, your duty you do,
The Lord has given rest to all,
As promised best, His mighty thrall.

Now return to your land and tent,
As Moses told, your hearts intent,
Keep God's command, His laws obey,
Love Him alone, walk in His way.

With blessings sent, they went their way,
In tents they dwelt, their hearts to sway,
In Gilead's land, their own domain,
As God had planned, where they'd remain.

But an altar raised by Jordan's shore,
Raised suspicions more and more,
The tribes of Israel gathered round,
War's threat was found, a troubling sound.

Phinehas, priest, with leaders wise,
To Gilead's east, with clear eyes,
Went to demand, explain their deed,

Why altar stand, to sow this seed?

Reuben, Gad, and Manasseh spoke,
With hearts provoked, their stance bespoke,
Not against the Lord did they rebel,
Their story to tell, in truth they quell.

Their altar's aim, not sacrifice,
Or burnt acclaim, but witness wise,
Between their kin, a sign to be,
In days within, for all to see.

And Israel pleased, no war pursued,
Their worries eased, their bonds renewed,
Blessings abound, God's hand displayed,
In unity found, peace was remade.

The altar's name, a bond to form,
Ed's witness came through the storm,
The Lord is God, forever known,
In every land, His glory shown.

TIME OF REFLECTION

A long time passed since God gave rest,
To Israel's land, their foes suppressed,
Joshua aged, his time at end,
Assembled all, his voice to send.

To Israel's leaders, young and old,
To judges wise, in stories told,
"I'm old," said he, "my days grow thin,
Yet look and see, the victories win.

God's hand, you've seen, against your foes,
His power keen, as history shows,
The nations there, by His command,
I've made you heir, in this very land.

The Lord your God will lead the way,
Expelling all, night and day,
With courage great, in His path tread,
Inscribed by fate, as the law you've read.

Don't intermix, with nations here,
Nor their gods fix, your hearts to cheer,
No worship stray, no oaths to share,
But Him obey, in devoted prayer.

Cling to the Lord, as you've done before,
His shield, His sword, in battles soar,
For though great kings and nations stand,
By His own wings, you'll rule the land.

One man will chase a thousand strong,
His foe will face, his courage long,
For God fights for you, as promised true,
His strength anew, will guide you through.

Be cautious now, love God above,
The solemn vow, your faith and love,
Don't turn aside, to nations near,
In sin confide, and their gods revere.

For if you stray and disobey,
His righteous way, and idols sway,
Then snares and traps, your path will mar,
Like thorns in gaps, they'll leave a scar.

As I depart from life's embrace,
Take to your heart, God's faithful grace,
His promises fulfilled, you see,
His words distilled, through history.

Yet heed my word of warning dire,
If idols stirred, God's holy fire,
His anger's blaze, will swiftly fall,
In darkened days, on one and all.

So keep the covenant true and pure,
Let love endure, your hearts secure,
For on this land, God's blessings rest,
But take a stand, and be truly blessed."

THE COVENANT STONE

Joshua summoned all Israel's clans,
Before God's presence, they took their stance,
Elders and leaders, judges and all,
Answering God's sovereign call.

"Your fathers dwelt across the flood,
In times of old, where idols stood,
I took Abraham, from that place,
Led him to Canaan's fruitful space.

His seed multiplied, Isaac his son,
Jacob and Esau, a tale begun,
To Esau, Seir's mountain I gave,
Yet Jacob's line in Egypt's wave.

I sent Moses and Aaron's might,
In Egypt's night, I caused a blight,
I led you out from Egypt's chain,
Through parted sea, your foes were slain.

Through wilderness you wandered far,
From Amorite's hand, I made you spar,
Into Canaan's land, I brought you near,
Your enemies' defeat, made clear.

Balak and Balaam's curse they sought,
But My will, against them, I tightly fought,
You crossed the Jordan, reached Jericho's wall,
Their strongholds fell, at my call.

I sent hornets to clear your way,
The Amorite kings I did sway,
I gave you lands and cities fair,
Vineyards and olives, beyond compare.

Now, fear the Lord, with heart sincere,
Serve Him alone, let idols disappear,
Choose today whom you will obey,
The gods of old, or God's righteous way.

As for me and my household, we stand,
To serve the Lord, a sacred band,
The people replied with hearts aglow,
"We'll follow the Lord, to Him we'll go."

Joshua warned of God's holy ire,
His burning fire, for those who tire,
But the people vowed, "We'll serve the Lord,"
Witnessed by heaven, their oath adored.

In Shechem's vale, a pact was made,
An oath displayed, foundations laid,
Joshua wrote in God's law book,
A covenant firm, the way to look.

A stone was raised, 'neath an oak's shade,
A witness made, by words displayed,
Joshua's voice echoed through the land,
Lest faith waver, by God's command.

Joshua's time came to an end,
An age well-spent, a faithful friend,
He was laid in Timnathserah's soil,
In Ephraim's mount, a place of toil.

Israel served God throughout those days,
Walking His ways, following His gaze,
Joseph's bones too found a home,
In Shechem's ground, 'neath starry dome.

Eleazar, Aaron's son, fell asleep,
On Ephraim's hill, his rest to keep,
Thus ended this era of old,
A story of faith, a tale of bold.

UNFINISHED CONQUESTS

After Joshua's passing, Israel's cry,
Asked who'd lead them, their foes to defy,
The Lord replied, "Judah shall rise,
I've given the land, his strength will suffice."

Judah and Simeon, as brothers in arms,
Fought 'gainst Canaanites, quelled their alarms,
Ten thousand men, in Bezek's fight,
The Lord gave victory, put foes to flight.

Adonibezek, a captive of old,
His thumbs and toes, were cruelly bold,
Seventy kings, he'd treated the same,
Retribution came, as God's righteous claim.

Jerusalem's walls by Judah's might fell,
The city was taken, its fate to tell,
They battled in mountain, valley, and more,
Bravely they fought, as in days of yore.

Hebron's conquest followed, strong and bold,
Caleb's promise, a prize untold,
Othniel arose, by courage driven,
Took the city, a prize God-given.

Achsah, his daughter, a bride to be,
She asked for land, a gracious plea,
Upper springs and lower too,
Caleb blessed her, her heart's desire grew.

Kenites of Moses, joined Judah's quest,
In wilderness dwelling, to find their rest,
With Judah and Simeon, they strove,
In Zephath they conquered, victory's rove.

Gaza, Askelon, and Ekron they took,
God's presence prevailed, they faced no rebuke,
But iron chariots in the valley's embrace,
Withheld full victory, in that challenging space.

To Caleb was Hebron, the promise held true,
Anak's sons ousted, the conquest they knew,
Yet tribes left pockets, foes to remain,
Tribute paid, not victory's gain.

Bethel's conquest by the house of Joseph,
Spies' cunning, a city's loss,
Luz became Luz once more,
Israel's strength they did endorse.

Manasseh and others, with gaps to show,
Failed to oust Canaanites, let them grow,
Amorites ruled, Dan's hand was pressed,
Tribute they paid, the weak confessed.

From Akrabbim's climb, the Amorite's might,
Prevailed 'gainst Dan, a valley in sight,
But Joseph's hand stronger, their tribute won,
Tribal stories, the land's battle spun.

So Israel, though strong, not fully free,
Allowed some foes, to dwell and be,
A mixture of conquest, and tribute paid,
Their journey through Canaan, a tale displayed.

THE ANGEL'S REBUKE

An angel of the Lord to Bochim came,
Rebuking Israel for not the same,
For they hadn't expelled the land's own kin,
Made treaties, altars stood, a grievous sin.

"I led you from Egypt," the angel cried,
To the land sworn to your fathers," he supplied,
"No pacts with the land's dwellers, make no peace,
Tear down altars, let evil cease."

"Why have you disobeyed?" the angel said,
Their gods as snares and thorns will spread,
But when these words the people heard,
They wept and offered sacrifices to the Lord.

Joshua's days ended, Israel took hold,
Each tribe received its heritage, as of old,
During Joshua's life, and the elders too,
Israel served God and to Him they were true.

But as this generation passed away,
A new one arose, that led astray,
They knew not God nor His wondrous deeds,
Evil they embraced, following pagan creeds.

They forsook the Lord, to idols turned,
Angering God, His wrath was earned,
He delivered them to enemies' might,
Spoilers, oppressors, a terrible plight.

Yet God showed mercy, raised judges' hand,
To save the people, from enemy's band,
But the cycle continued, time and again,
Israel sinned, then sought God to remain.

Though judges arose and delivered the land,
Israel turned to idols, a cycle so grand,
God's anger flared, His patience worn thin,
Israel's transgressions had led them to sin.

The covenant broken, commands ignored,
Anger and punishment, Israel's reward,
The nations they should've driven out,
Remained in the land, a test, no doubt.

God's purpose revealed, to test and prove,
If Israel would keep His ways, truth they'd move,
A generation failed, and the nations stayed,
Not swiftly driven out, God's plan portrayed.

PAT DENIM

THE STRONGMAN'S DOWNFALL

Israel, tested by nations left in place,
To prove their faith, their hearts' true grace,
Those unaware of Canaan's wars of old,
Were left, their loyalty and strength to mold.

Philistines, Canaanites, and Sidonians too,
The Hivites in Lebanon, all this crew,
They stayed to test if Israel would obey,
The Lord's commands, to worship and stay.

But Israel mingled with these nations' kin,
Took wives and gods, a deadly sin,
They turned from God, served idols and more,
Baalim and groves, their hearts did ignore.

God's anger flared, His patience waned,
Chushanrishathaim, king of Mesopotamia reigned,
For eight long years, Israel served in shame,
Then cried to God, and a deliverer He named.

Othniel, Caleb's kin, by Spirit's power led,
He judged and fought, by God's hand he was fed,
Forty years of rest the land then saw,
Till Othniel passed away, God's chosen law.

Again Israel fell, in evil's grip ensnared,
Eglon of Moab, God's judgment shared,
With Ammon and Amalek, he waged his fight,
Israel's palm city he took with might.

Eighteen years, Israel bowed to Moab's rule,
Till cries went up, deliverance the call,
Ehud arose, left-handed, wise and bold,
A double-edged dagger his secret hold.

To Eglon he went with a present in hand,
A secret errand, a message from God's strand,
A blade to his belly, his lifeblood did drain,
Israel's deliverance, a new dawn to gain.

Ehud escaped, the doors he locked tight,
His lord was dead, his plan took flight,
Trumpet sound, on Ephraim's mount he blew,
Israel rallied, to Moab's defeat they flew.

Ten thousand slain, Moab's force put to rest,
Subdued by Israel, God's will they'd expressed,
Eighty years of rest for the land and its kin,
Shamgar arose, Philistines he'd win.

With ox goad, six hundred Philistines fell,
Shamgar's might and courage, a story to tell,
Judges in succession, God's hand revealed,
Cycles of sin and deliverance, Israel's fate sealed.

CUNNING DEED

In Israel's days of waywardness once more,
Ehud's passing led them to a grievous door,
Jabin, the Canaanite king, held his sway,
Sisera, his captain, caused Israel to obey.

Nine hundred iron chariots, a fearful might,
Oppressed God's people, darkness and blight,
Twenty years of sorrow, they endured,
Till their cries reached God, their voices assured.

Deborah, a prophetess, rose to lead,
Judging with wisdom, in their time of need,
Under a palm tree, her judgment was sought,
She called Barak, God's plans she brought.

Barak of Kedesh, Deborah's command received,
Ten thousand men he gathered, he believed,
The river Kishon, the place of the fight,
Sisera and his chariots would take their flight.

Deborah's assurance echoed in the air,
God's promise of victory, their hope to share,
Barak descended with his troops in tow,
Sisera and his army met their final blow.

The Lord's hand was mighty, Sisera's host fell,
Chariots and soldiers met their judgment's knell,
Sisera fled, a tent he sought as his shield,
Jael, Heber's wife, had plans concealed.

She offered refreshment, put him at ease,
Then drove a nail through his temple with ease,
Barak pursued, led by Jael's call,
And Sisera's fate was revealed to all.

God's power prevailed, Jabin's rule was ceased,
Israel was delivered, their enemies deceased,
For a time they prospered, free from their foe,
God's hand was with them, His strength in tow.

FREED FROM CHAINS

Deborah and Barak sang on that victorious day,
Praising the Lord for Israel's triumphant way,
The people offered themselves willingly to fight,
Against oppression, they stood with all their might.

Kings and princes, give heed to my song,
I will sing praise to the Lord all day long,
As the Lord marched from Seir to Edom's field,
Earth trembled, heavens poured, His power revealed.

Mountains melted, Sinai bowed before His might,
In Shamgar's days, highways were empty, no sight,
But I, Deborah, arose, a mother for Israel,
Leading them to victory, breaking oppression's spell.

New gods they chose, war filled the gates,
No shield or spear seen among Israel's fates,
Yet the governors stepped forth willingly,
Blessing the Lord, their courage shining brightly.

Judges and leaders, speak with authority,
Rehearse God's acts, His righteous sincerity,
People gather at the gates, stories unfold,
God's victories celebrated, His glory told.

Awake, Deborah, sing your song anew,
Arise, Barak, as the leader so true,
Dominion granted over nobles and might,
The Lord's hand prevailing, in His holy light.

Roots from Ephraim, Benjamin's force,
Machir's governors, Zebulun's course,
Princes of Issachar joined the fight,
Barak sent on foot, with courage to ignite.

Reuben's divisions, thoughts deep within,
Gilead and Dan, in battles to win,
Zebulun and Naphtali, lives they gave,
High places of the field, their courage engrave.

Kings of Canaan fought, Megiddo's shore,
Heaven itself joined the battle's roar,
Kishon's river swept away their might,
Strength was trampled, victory was in sight.

Horsehoofs broken, prancing horses still,
Meroz cursed for not aiding God's will,
Blessed is Jael, her courage and might,
Above all women, in the tent's light.

Water to milk, a lordly feast,
Her hand on the nail, the hammer released,
Sisera's head struck, his power undone,
He fell at her feet, victory won.

Sisera's mother, peered out through the lattice,
Why's his chariot late? Her question, a crisis,
Wise women answered with jests so wry,
Damsels for prey, a colorful cry.

Let all God's enemies perish, oh Lord,
Let them who love You rise and be restored,
As the sun in its strength, shining so bright,
And Israel had rest for forty years, a blessed sight.

IMPOVERISHED HEARTS

The children of Israel again turned astray,
Into the hands of Midian, the Lord let them sway,
For seven years they suffered under Midian's might,
Seeking refuge in mountains, caves, hidden from sight.

Midian, Amalek, and eastern foes,
Raided their crops, destruction they chose,
Leaving Israel with naught, sustenance none,
As grasshoppers they came, countless as the sun.

Greatly impoverished, Israel cried out in pain,
To the Lord they prayed, seeking relief from this chain,
A prophet was sent to remind them once more,
Of God's faithfulness, their history's core.

An angel appeared to Gideon one day,
While he threshed wheat, hidden away,
"Mighty man of valor," the angel proclaimed,
God was with him, Gideon's destiny framed.

Gideon questioned, "Why has this befallen us,
Where are the miracles our fathers told us?"
The Lord replied, "Go forth in your might,
I send you to save Israel, dispel the blight."

Gideon hesitated, doubting his worth,
His family poor, least in his father's hearth,
But the Lord reassured, "I will be with you,
Smite the Midianites, your purpose you'll pursue."

Gideon sought a sign, his faith to increase,
The angel's presence, he longed to release,
He offered a present, a kid and cakes prepared,
Fire consumed them, a sign divinely declared.

Acknowledging the angel, Gideon was filled with dread,
Seeing an angel of the Lord face to face he said,
"Alas, O Lord God! I may surely die,"
But the Lord calmed him, "Peace, don't be shy."

An altar Gideon built to the Lord that day,
Jehovahshalom, in Ophrah it would stay,
Then the Lord commanded, another task at hand,
Topple Baal's altar, in the ordered land.

Gideon obeyed, though fear gripped his heart,
He did it by night, from society apart,
The city awoke, the altar was down,
The second bullock offered, a new dawn's crown.

The men were outraged, demanding his death,
For casting down Baal's altar, taking his breath,
But Joash, Gideon's father, defended his son,
Challenging Baal to prove himself, everyone.

Joash named Gideon Jerubbaal that day,
Let Baal plead, his altar's dismay,
Midianites and Amalekites gathered in force,
In the valley of Jezreel, their paths did course.

The Spirit of the Lord upon Gideon fell,
He blew a trumpet, Abiezer he did compel,
Messengers were sent through Manasseh's lands,
Asher, Zebulun, Naphtali, they joined hands.

Gideon asked the Lord, seeking to know,
If Israel would be saved, as the Lord's words show,
He placed a fleece on the floor overnight,
Dew only on the fleece, the rest was dry in sight.

Gideon asked again, a sign for his peace,
This time, dew on the ground, the fleece dry's lease,
God answered his tests, his faith to uplift,
Guiding Gideon's steps, despite every rift.

TORCHLIGHT STRATEGY

At the well of Harod, Gideon and his band,
Pitched their camp, ready to take a stand,
Midianites were on the northern side,
In the valley, by the hill, they did abide.

The Lord spoke to Gideon, "Too many are here,
Lest vainglory in victory they rear,
Proclaim to those fearful to depart and flee,
Twenty-two thousand left, ten thousand to be."

Yet still too many, the Lord declared anew,
At the water's test, He'd reveal the true,
Three hundred lapped, hand to mouth, alert,
While the rest knelt, quenching their thirst in the dirt.

With three hundred, Gideon would prevail,
The Midianites' might, they would curtail,
He sent the rest home, their trumpets they bore,
Midian's camp below, they stood on the floor.

The Lord told Gideon to descend without fright,
If fear gripped him, go with Phurah's light,
They heard a dream, barley bread's mighty fall,
Gideon's sword, God's deliverance call.

Strengthened by the dream, Gideon returned,
Worshipping God, his heart's fire burned,
Dividing his force into companies three,
With trumpets and torches, a plan set free.

"Look on me," he said, "and follow my cue,
When I blow the trumpet, you shall blow too,
Declare, 'The sword of the Lord and Gideon's might,'"
Three hundred men stood, prepared for the fight.

In the middle watch, the trumpets they blew,
Breaking the pitchers, the torchlight they drew,
The shout of their voices, a sword's piercing sound,
The Midianites trembled, chaos unbound.

Panic spread through the Midianite host,
They turned on each other, a chaotic ghost,
Bethshittah, Zererath, and Abelmeholah they fled,
From Naphtali, Asher, and Manasseh, pursuit led.

Gideon sent messengers to Ephraim's land,
To take Bethbarah and Jordan in hand,
Princes Oreb and Zeeb met their doom,
As Gideon's victory sealed Midian's tomb.

TROUBLED HOUSE

The men of Ephraim, with words so sharp,
Questioned Gideon, their anger did spark,
"Why didn't you call us to join the fray,
Against Midian, on that fateful day?"

Gideon responded, humility in his tone,
"Compared to Ephraim's strength, mine's not known,
Is not Ephraim's gleaning worth much more,
Than Abiezer's vintage from days of yore?"

He pacified them, their anger subsiding,
Their shared mission united, their anger hiding,
Gideon pressed on, pursuing the foe,
Three hundred men faint, but courage did show.

To Succoth he came, asked for bread and aid,
For his men who were weary, the request was made,
But the princes denied, refused him with pride,
Gideon vowed vengeance, God on his side.

To Penuel he went, made the same plea,
For bread for his men, to sustain them to be free,
But Penuel's response, like Succoth's did stand,
When Gideon returned, he'd tear their tower's grand.

He reached Karkor, where Midian did remain,
Their host of fifteen thousand, all that did remain,
With torches and trumpets, he struck in the night,
Zebah and Zalmunna fled from the fight.

Gideon pursued, the two kings he found,
Zebah and Zalmunna, in whom pride was bound,
With thorns and briers, the men of Succoth he taught,
The consequences of their selfish thought.

The tower of Penuel, Gideon tore down,
Slew the men of the city, a king with a frown,
He questioned the kings, who were slain at Tabor,
Resembling kings, a grim, tragic labor.

His request for his son, met hesitation and fear,
Yet Gideon obeyed, the kings' end was near,
Israel offered rulership, but Gideon refused,
Only the Lord's rule, he firmly deduced.

Golden earrings, a request to fulfill,
From the Midianites' plunder, the wealth to distill,
He fashioned an ephod, a symbol of might,
But Israel strayed, a snare in their sight.

Midian was subdued, their reign at an end,
Israel flourished, on God they depend,
Forty years of peace followed Gideon's days,
But soon, their faith faltered, a darkening haze.

Gideon's life came to an end,
Threescore and ten sons, his legacy did blend,
His house became troubled, discord arose,
Abimelech's rise, the nation's woes.

Gideon was buried with honor and pride,
In the sepulcher of Joash, where ancestors reside,
Israel turned to Baal, away from the Lord,
Gideon's goodness, they soon ignored.

THE TOWER'S REFUGE

Abimelech, Jerubbaal's son, arose with might,
To Shechem he went, his plan to incite,
To his mother's kin he spoke, in earnest plea,
"Should one rule or all, let my reign be."

His kin whispered his name in Shechem's ears,
To Abimelech they turned, dismissing their fears,
They gave him silver, he hired men so light,
To follow his lead, to join in the fight.

Back to Ophrah he went, his heart full of hate,
Slew Jerubbaal's sons, met a terrible fate,
Jotham survived, in secret he hid,
The youngest son spared, by Providence's bid.

Men of Shechem crowned him, king of their land,
By the pillar in Shechem, they took their stand,
Jotham's voice rang out, from Gerizim on high,
A parable told, a truth he'd imply.

The trees sought a king, each in its own way,
Olive, fig, and vine had words to convey,
The bramble, least worthy, rose to the task,
But its shadow brought fire, destruction unasked.

Jotham condemned, their choice he reproved,
The blood of Jerubbaal's sons never removed,
The evil between them, God's wrath it did spark,
Upon Abimelech and Shechem, it left its mark.

Liers in wait ambushed, Abimelech was told,
They robbed on the mountains, bold and cold,
Gaal and his brethren took Shechem's side,
In revelry and curses, they did confide.

Gaal questioned Abimelech, scorn in his voice,
Challenging his rule, a reckless choice,
Zebul's anger flared, in secret he sent word,
To Abimelech, danger had stirred.

At night, they set an ambush, a clever scheme,
In four companies, they planned to redeem,
Gaal's challenge met with battle's fierce flame,
Abimelech pursued, marked by his name.

At Arumah he dwelt, Zebul his aid,
Gaal and his brethren's rule he forbade,
Once more they clashed, the city they fought,
Shechem fell, destruction was wrought.

The tower's men took refuge, strong and tall,
A woman's act, a millstone to fall,
Abimelech's end, a painful demise,
By his own armorbearer, his life met its ties.

Israel saw his death, scattered far and wide,
Justice was served, God's hand couldn't hide,
The wickedness of Abimelech, he paid the cost,
The curse of Jotham fulfilled, all was not lost.

IDOLS AND ENEMIES

After Abimelech's rule, Tola did rise,
A man of Issachar, wise and wise,
In Shamir he dwelt, in Ephraim's mount,
Judged Israel for years, a righteous account.

Twenty-three years he held his reign,
Then passed away, his work not in vain,
Buried in Shamir, his resting place,
A judge of Israel, in God's embrace.

Next came Jair, Gileadite strong,
Twenty-two years he ruled, just and long,
Thirty sons he had, riding colts of ass,
Cities thirty, a legacy to amass.

Havothjair they're called, unto this day,
In Gilead's land, where they held sway,
Jair was buried in Camon's abode,
A judge of Israel, on history's road.

But again Israel strayed, turned from the Lord,
Served foreign gods, a sin abhorred,
Baalim, Ashtaroth, and others they chose,
God's anger ignited, His judgment arose.

Philistines and Ammon, their enemies strong,
Into their hands, God's people did throng,
Eighteen years of oppression they bore,
Tribulations and trials, their hearts were sore.

Ammon crossed Jordan, against Judah and more,
Israel's distress deepened, a troubling roar,
The people cried out, their voices in prayer,
Confessed their wrongs, their sins laid bare.

The Lord spoke, "Did I not save you before,
From Egyptians and Amorites, conflict galore?
Though you forsook Me, and served other gods,
Still I delivered you from their hostile odds."

"You've turned away, your idols embraced,
No longer will I rescue, by My grace,
Cry to the gods you've chosen, let them save,
In your time of trouble, the help you crave."

Israel repented, their sins they bemoaned,
Stranger gods discarded, to God's ways they turned,
His heart was moved by their misery's plight,
Their earnest remorse, their plea for His light.

The children of Ammon amassed in Gilead,
Israel gathered at Mizpeh, hearts not sad,
Gilead's people sought a leader to defend,
A head over all, their strife to attend.

TRAGIC VOW FULFILLED

Jephthah, the Gileadite, strong and bold,
A mighty man of valor, we are told,
Born to a harlot, yet Gilead's blood ran through,
His heritage and lineage true.

Gilead's wife bore sons, and with disdain,
They cast out Jephthah, their actions profane,
"You're a son of a strange woman," they sneered,
Inheritance denied, his fate appeared.

Jephthah fled to the land of Tob, alone,
Vain men gathered around, a force he'd known,
Ammon made war, against Israel they rose,
Gilead's elders sought him, foes to oppose.

"Lead us against Ammon," they earnestly implored,
But Jephthah remembered how he was ignored,
"Why come to me now?" he questioned their plea,
"When you treated me so unjustly?"

Yet they urged him to lead, their captain to be,
In battle against Ammon, their hope was he,
"If I lead, and the Lord grants victory to me,
Will I be your head?" Jephthah asked firmly.

They agreed, "The Lord be witness," they swore,
Jephthah became their head, his leadership they bore,
Before the Lord in Mizpeh, he stood to pray,
Uttering his words, seeking God's way.

Messengers sent to Ammon's king, a quest,
"Why war against us?" Jephthah addressed,
The king replied, citing ancient land's claim,
Demanding restoration, peace without blame.

Jephthah countered, with historical facts,
Israel didn't harm Moab's or Ammon's tracks,
Recalling the journey, their wilderness stride,
Passing Edom and Moab, where they did bide.

Amorites' lands they gained by God's hand,
From Arnon to Jabbok, all the land's expanse,
The Lord dispossessed the Amorites in fight,
Israel claimed it by God's might.

"Why do you now seek to possess what's ours,
Given by Chemosh, your god, in those hours?
The Lord our God will drive out the rest,
As He has in the past, for our conquest."

Jephthah challenged, "Are you greater, say,
Than Balak of Moab, in his display?
Three hundred years we've dwelt by Arnon's side,
Why didn't you reclaim then, in pride?"

He pleaded innocence, unjust was the war,
God the Judge between them, he implored,
Ammon's king, unmoved, ignored his plea,
The Spirit of the Lord came upon Jephthah, free.

He passed through Gilead, to Manasseh's land,
Then to Mizpeh, his people to command,
He vowed to the Lord, in fervent plea,
"If Ammon falls, a burnt offering will be."

Jephthah engaged Ammon, the Lord's hand at play,
He smote them from Aroer, on that day,
Through the cities, the plain, with power, with might,
Ammon subdued, Israel's triumph in sight.

Returning home, his daughter met him in cheer,
With timbrels and dances, no cause for fear,
His only child, a joy in his eyes,
But Jephthah's vow brought tears and sighs.

He rent his clothes, in grief he cried,
"Alas, my daughter!" his sorrow implied,
His oath to the Lord, he could not withdraw,
His heart heavy with sorrow, a solemn awe.

His daughter accepted, his vow she embraced,
God's vengeance achieved, Ammon's disgrace,
She asked for two months, on mountains to weep,
Bewailing her virginity, her promise to keep.

Jephthah granted her request, his heart torn,
She went with her friends, her grief to mourn,
Returning after two months' lament,
He fulfilled his vow, her sacrifice meant.

Thus, a custom arose, for years to last,
Daughters of Israel mourned, memories of the past,
Jephthah's daughter, a sacrifice true,
A story of faith, a vow to renew.

THE JORDAN CROSSING

The men of Ephraim, angered and bold,
Confronted Jephthah, their grievances told,
"Why fight Ammon without us?" they cried,
"We'll burn your house, our fury won't hide."

Jephthah responded, explaining his plight,
When he called them, they didn't take flight,
Facing Ammon alone, he took the stand,
The Lord's hand brought victory to his hand.

"Why now oppose me?" he questioned in ire,
Ephraim's anger, a situation dire,
Jephthah gathered Gilead's men to the fight,
Against Ephraim's forces, fierce and bright.

They took the Jordan crossings in control,
Ephraimites who fled paid a toll,
To discern their allegiance, a test devised,
"Say Shibboleth," they were advised.

But Ephraim's speech couldn't form the sound,
"Sibboleth" from their lips, they found,
At the passages of Jordan, many fell,
Forty-two thousand, the tale does tell.

Jephthah ruled Israel, six years in reign,
His judgment and leadership took the strain,
He passed away, in Gilead he's laid,
A leader's legacy, his mark displayed.

Ibzan of Bethlehem, next in line,
Judged Israel, his leadership divine,
Thirty sons and daughters, abroad he sent,
With foreign daughters, their lives he blent.

Seven years of rule, then Ibzan's time ceased,
He was buried in Bethlehem's peace,
Elon, a Zebulonite, then took his stand,
Ten years he governed, with wisdom grand.

In Aijalon's country, his resting place,
Elon passed on, his legacy to trace,
Abdon, Hillel's son, from Pirathon came,
Forty sons and nephews, he gained in fame.

Seventy ass colts, in glory rode,
Judged Israel eight years, in justice he strode,
Abdon's reign ended, his rule well-known,
Buried in Ephraim, his journey full-grown.

A FEARSOME SIGHT

The Israelites again did what was wrong,
In the Lord's sight, they didn't stand strong,
Delivered to Philistines' grip so tight,
Forty years of suffering took its flight.

From Zorah came Manoah, of Danite kin,
Barren was his wife, their story begins,
An angel appeared, this message to tell,
A son would be born, a Nazarite, he'd excel.

No wine, strong drink, or unclean food to consume,
His hair uncut, in God's service would bloom,
To start Israel's rescue from Philistines' might,
A Nazarite's mission, to bring forth the light.

The woman shared this vision of divine,
With her husband Manoah, a message to align,
She told him of the angel's fearsome sight,
His countenance like God's, shining bright.

Manoah prayed to see the man again,
For guidance on raising this special son's reign,
God listened to his voice, answered his plea,
The angel returned, a wondrous scene to see.

Guidelines for the child's life were set,
No vine's produce, no wine to be met,
No unclean food, a Nazarite true,
The woman and man must follow this too.

Manoah offered to prepare a feast,
The angel declined, his mission released,
He revealed his nature, a secret untold,
Manoah and wife watched the marvel unfold.

An altar they raised, sacrifices made,
As the flame rose, in awe they stayed,
The angel ascended in the fiery light,
Manoah and wife fell, their faces white.

No more did the angel appear in their sight,
His mission fulfilled, vanished from light,
Realization struck, Manoah's heart's swell,
"We've seen God, surely now we'll farewell."

But his wife brought reason, her voice wise,
God's acceptance of offerings, no demise,
Blessings were theirs, this special son's start,
Samson, they named him, a story to impart.

In the camp of Dan, Samson grew in grace,
The Spirit of the Lord would guide his pace,
Between Zorah and Eshtaol, the camp's embrace,
A hero in the making, in God's chosen place.

THE BETRAYAL

Samson journeyed down to Timnath's land,
Where a Philistine woman he saw so grand,
He told his parents of his heart's desire,
"Get her for me to wed," his burning fire.

But his parents questioned, "Why this choice?
Among our people, find a bride's voice.
Is it right to take from the uncircumcised,
A wife, and be by Philistines disguised?"

Samson replied, "She pleases me, it's true,
A path guided by my heart's view."
Unbeknownst to them, God's plan was in motion,
Using Samson to stir Philistine commotion.

The Spirit of the Lord, mighty and grand,
Came upon Samson, fierce as a lion's stand,
He tore the beast apart with strength untamed,
A secret of triumph, his parents remained.

He returned for the woman, a feast he made,
Thirty companions joined, a lively brigade,
A riddle he posed, a challenge profound,
"Tell it in seven days, rewards will abound."

"From the eater came forth meat," he declared,
"From the strong, sweetness," his riddle bared,
Three days passed, they couldn't discern,
The meaning behind his words, the puzzle to learn.

On the seventh day, they turned to his wife,
"Entice your husband to share the riddle's life,
Or your family's house will meet its pyre's fate,
For answers to the riddle we impatiently await."

She wept, and Samson's heart she did sway,
She pleaded for the riddle, night and day,
He finally relented, shared the secret within,
The riddle's truth to her, a Philistine.

At sunset, the men of the city came near,
With the answer in hand, they taunted with jeer,
"What's sweeter than honey, what's stronger than beast?"
"If you hadn't plowed with my heifer," his anger increased.

With the Spirit upon him, fierce and unchained,
To Ashkelon he went, where lives were stained,
Thirty men he struck down, their garments he gave,
To those who'd solved the riddle, his fury did pave.

In anger, he left, returned to his kin,
His wife, given away, to another within,
A tale of riddles, honey, and might,
Samson's story unfolds, in God's guiding light.

FIERY RETRIBUTION

In wheat harvest's time, Samson's visit came,
To his wife, he went with a kid, love's flame,
"I'll go to her chamber," he planned to say,
But her father blocked his path, led him astray.

"I thought you hated her," her father claimed,
So, her companion's hand, his daughter he named,
"Take her younger sister, fairer in sight,
Instead of the one you sought with love's light."

Samson mused, "I'll be blameless, it seems,
When I unleash the foxes, set aglow their dreams,"
With firebrands, he paired tails, three hundred they'd be,
Into Philistine's fields, he sent them running free.

Shocks of corn, vineyards, and olives met their fate,
In fiery blaze, they perished, a devastating state,
The Philistines cried out, "Who's done this to us?"
"Samson, the Timnite's son-in-law," their voices thus.

They burned her and her father, in revenge's fire,
Samson declared, "Retribution is my desire,
I'll avenge this act, then my hand will cease,"
With great slaughter, he struck, and went to find peace.

To the rock Etam's top, Samson withdrew,
The Philistines encamped, their anger grew,
"Why are you against us?" Judah inquired,
"To bind Samson," they answered, their voices tired.

Three thousand from Judah to Samson did speak,
"Philistines rule us, you've made our situation bleak,
Why have you provoked them to this harsh state?"
Samson responded, his vengeance he'd not abate.

"As they did to me, so to them I've done,
Retaliation's path, by their actions spun,"
"We came to bind you," Judah then said,
But Samson requested, "Swear not to see me dead."

"We'll bind you, deliver you," their promise was made,
With new cords, they bound him, to the Philistines' aid,
As they brought him to Lehi, they shouted in glee,
But the Spirit of the Lord set Samson free.

Cords turned to flax, burnt by fiery might,
His bands fell away, his hands took their flight,
With a jawbone of an ass, he struck down a horde,
A thousand men fell to his blade, their end soared.

Samson exclaimed, "With this jawbone I've slain,
A thousand men, heaps upon heaps, pain by pain,"
After his triumph, the jawbone he threw,
Ramathlehi, the place's name, anew.

Thirst overtaking, he called on the Lord,
For water to quench, a plea he outpoured,
God's answer brought water from jawbone's place,
Revived, he named it Enhakkore, God's grace.

Twenty years, Samson judged, amid Philistines' reign,
A life marked by strength, battles fought in disdain,
A complex tale of power, vengeance, and might,
Samson's legacy shines through darkness and light.

COLLAPSE OF THE TEMPLE

To Gaza Samson went, a harlot he found,
Into her chamber, desire unbound,
The Gazites learned of his arrival near,
In ambush they lay, their plan to appear.

All night they waited, in silence they lay,
Morning's light would bring forth their prey,
But Samson rose at midnight's chime,
Took the city's gates, a feat most sublime.

He placed them on his shoulders, bar and all,
Carried them uphill, a task quite tall,
In the valley of Sorek, a woman he adored,
Delilah her name, his heart she explored.

Philistine lords approached Delilah's door,
They sought to know Samson's strength, explore,
"Entice him," they said, "and learn his might,
We'll give you silver, a fortune so bright."

Delilah inquired, "Tell me your strength's core,
How could I bind you, leave you weak and sore?"
Samson answered, "With un-dried green cords, you see,
Bound with them, I'd be weak, like a man, not free."

PAT DENIM

With cords she bound him, the plan she tried,
But he snapped them like threads, strength undenied,
Again, with new ropes, she sought to ensnare,
Yet they, too, were broken, his power laid bare.

Seven locks of his hair, Delilah did weave,
Fastened them tight, her intent to deceive,
But once more he broke free, strength unimpaired,
A secret retained, his secret strength shared.

With persistence, Delilah pressed day by day,
Samson's vexed soul had no more to say,
In her arms, he disclosed his secret's deep core,
A Nazarite's vow, his hair, strength's store.

Delilah informed the Philistine lords of his truth,
They paid her silver, the secret of his youth,
As Samson slumbered, his hair she did shave,
His strength left him, captive to their brave.

Blinded and bound, to Gaza he was led,
A prisoner's fate, filled with pain and dread,
He toiled as a grinder, confined in disgrace,
A fallen hero, captured in their chase.

The Philistines rejoiced, their god they praised,
For Samson's downfall, their enemy's daze,
They gathered for a sacrifice grand,
To Dagon, their god, across the land.

In their merriment, they called for Samson's game,
From prison they brought him, a pawn in their aim,
Between the pillars, he stood that day,
Samson, once mighty, now under their sway.

He asked the lad to guide his hands with care,
To touch the pillars, their strength to bear,
With a prayer to the Lord, he called for might,
To avenge his eyes, his final fight.

He pushed the pillars with all his force,
The house collapsed, a mighty discourse,
Lords and people, dead in their pride,
Samson's revenge, death's toll they'd bide.

His kin came to claim his lifeless form,
Between Zorah and Eshtaol, his resting norm,
Twenty years he judged Israel's plight,
A legacy left in strength's endless fight.

THE MISSING SILVER

In Mount Ephraim dwelt a man named Micah,
A tale of idols, priests, and a sacred jar,
His mother's silver, taken in secret flight,
Brought guilt to his heart, but also delight.

"Eleven hundred shekels," she had cursed,
A secret revealed, her anger dispersed,
Micah confessed, the silver was his hold,
Blessings from his mother, the story was told.

Restored was the silver, to her delight,
Dedicated to the Lord, set right,
Yet she took two hundred shekels, the story goes,
For images and idols, her devotion chose.

In Micah's house, gods found their abode,
An ephod, teraphim, worship bestowed,
A son consecrated, to serve as priest,
A family's devotion, a faith increased.

In those days of Israel, without a king,
Each acted as they saw fit, doing their thing,
A Levite from Bethlehem, a young man did roam,
He journeyed to Ephraim, looking for a home.

To Micah's house, the Levite found his way,
From Bethlehem to Ephraim, led astray,
Micah welcomed him, offered silver and bread,
A father and a priest, the Levite was led.

With contentment, the Levite joined their clan,
As one of Micah's sons, their journey began,
Consecrated by Micah, the young man's role,
As priest in Micah's house, he took control.

Micah's joy grew, his heart filled with ease,
With a Levite as priest, his faith to please,
He believed the Lord's goodness he'd see,
Having a Levite to serve and be.

DANCING WITH SHADOWS

In those days, Israel lacked a king's sway,
Danites sought land, their inheritance's delay,
Five men were chosen to scout and spy,
From Zorah and Eshtaol, they prepared to fly.

To Mount Ephraim, their steps were led,
To Micah's house, where they found a bed,
The Levite's voice recognized they well,
Questions arose as secrets they'd tell.

The Levite explained how Micah's ways went,
Hired as priest, a role for which he was sent,
The Danites sought counsel from the divine,
Seeking guidance, their path to define.

"Go in peace," the priest's words held,
A blessing bestowed, their hearts upheld,
The men then departed for Laish's shore,
A people at ease, quiet, and secure.

No magistrate ruled, they lived without care,
Far from the Zidonians, their lives rare,
News they brought back to Zorah and its kin,
Prompting questions, thoughts and plans within.

"Arise, let's go up," their voices cried,
Secure land they saw, none could hide,
God had given it to them, they believed,
A promising place, they felt relieved.

Six hundred armed men, Danites strong,
From Zorah and Eshtaol, they moved along,
To Kirjathjearim, they pitched their camp,
A new name they gave, as if from a lamp.

In Mount Ephraim, they reached Micah's space,
The Levite's house, where he found his place,
Five spies revealed the idols within,
To their brethren, they brought the tale of sin.

With weapons of war, six hundred did stand,
At the gate's entrance, their position grand,
The spies took the idols, images of wrong,
With the Levite priest, the scene played along.

"What do you?" the priest did question,
But the Danites desired his priestly confession,
They offered him status, priesthood for a tribe,
A tempting offer, he couldn't describe.

Gladness filled his heart, he joined their quest,
With the idols and priest, they moved with zest,
As they left Micah's, with the idols in tow,
Little ones and cattle before them did go.

Yet Micah's neighbors cried out with might,
"What aileth thee?" their voices took flight,
Micah lamented, "You took what I made,
My gods, my priest, for what have they paid?"

But the Danites moved on, too strong for a fight,
Micah returned to his home that night,
The idols in hand, they reached Laish's shore,
The city they attacked, its end to explore.

With sword's edge they struck, the city aflame,
No deliverer appeared, no rescue came,
A city they built, Dan was its name,
Replacing Laish, a new path to claim.

An idol they set, the Levite as priest,
For the tribe of Dan, a role that won't cease,
Micah's image found its new abode,
Until Shiloh's house of God was bestowed.

DARK SECRETS

In those days, without a king to lead,
A Levite resided on Ephraim's heed,
He took a concubine from Bethlehem's stead,
But she betrayed him, her virtue did bleed.

She fled to her father's home in despair,
Four months she stayed, in sorrow and care,
Her husband pursued, with servant and mare,
To bring her back, their love to repair.

To her father's house they came, and he,
Welcomed them warmly, joyous and free,
Three days they spent in cheerful glee,
Eating and drinking, in company.

On the fourth day, as they planned to depart,
The father urged them, a morsel to start,
They lingered and stayed, the day's end to chart,
Again the father persuaded with heart.

The fifth day arrived, they were eager to go,
But the father implored them, their journey to slow,
They lingered once more, for hours to flow,
Till the day turned to dusk, their pace set to grow.

Near Jebus they reached, the sun sinking low,
The servant suggested, a city to know,
But the Levite refused, a city of foe,
They aimed for Gibeah, where they'd go.

Past Gibeah they journeyed, the sun now set,
They turned aside, their lodging to get,
But in Gibeah's streets, no host to be met,
No one offered shelter, no place to be set.

Then an old man came, from the field he did roam,
From Ephraim's mount, he found them alone,
He offered them refuge, his kindness was shown,
Asses were fed, a place to call home.

As evening came, they made merry and dine,
But the city's men, perverse and malign,
Besieged the house, with intent most unkind,
Demanding the Levite, desires intertwined.

The master resisted, pleaded with plea,
Suggested his daughter, the concubine, be,
Sacrificed to their lust, their torment set free,
But spared the Levite from their wicked spree.

The men refused, the woman they seized,
Abused her all night, as darkness was eased,
At dawn she returned, her suffering appeased,
At her husband's door, fallen and seized.

He urged her to rise, to journey anew,
But no response came, her life's flame withdrew,
He placed her on his ass, sorrow imbued,
To his place he went, her life he'd eschew.

At his house, he took a gruesome task in hand,
A knife and his concubine, bones divided on demand,
Twelve pieces sent forth, across the land,
A horrifying act, by his own hand.

The sight was shocking, unheard of before,
From Egypt's exodus to this day's door,
Israel had never witnessed such gore,
They pondered and counseled, the truth to explore.

ENDLESS NIGHT

The children of Israel united as one,
From Dan to Beersheba, the assembly begun,
In Mizpeh, they gathered, under the sun,
To address the wickedness, the evil that's done.

Four hundred thousand, to battle they came,
From each tribe they marched, with swords aflame,
The Levite spoke, revealing the shame,
How Gibeah's men had sullied their name.

The tribe of Benjamin, upon hearing the plea,
Refused to heed, to set the captives free,
They rallied to Gibeah, prepared for a spree,
Against their own kin, a fierce enemy.

The Benjamites fought, against Israel's might,
On the first day, twenty-two thousand's plight,
Israel wept, in sorrowful sight,
But God's guidance came, shining bright.

On the second day, the battle renewed,
Eighteen thousand fell, their fate eschewed,
Israel sought counsel, their faith renewed,
God promised success, with courage imbued.

Liars in wait were set, a strategic ploy,
Israel pressed on, their purpose to deploy,
The Benjamites thought they'd conquer with joy,
But a flame and smoke rose, destroying their buoy.

In confusion, the Benjamites turned to flee,
Israel pursued them, from bondage to free,
They fell by the thousands, a tragic spree,
Till only six hundred escaped, by the sea.

Benjamin was defeated, cities laid low,
Their resistance was shattered, their strength in tow,
The men of Israel, their anger aglow,
Brought justice and vengeance, a powerful blow.

Cities set ablaze, their conquest complete,
Benjamin's strength broken, their fate was replete,
The battle was fierce, the outcome bittersweet,
But justice prevailed, the wicked faced defeat.

SIN IN THE STREETS

The men of Israel, their oath held strong,
No daughters for Benjamin, they did belong,
They wept before God, a sorrowful throng,
One tribe lacked, a grievous wrong.

They built an altar, offerings raised,
For the tribe of Benjamin, ways they phased,
A solemn vow had been embraced,
No daughters for them, the oath encased.

But they pondered and sought a way to amend,
For the vow they took, they wished to suspend,
Jabesh-gilead untouched, they'd send,
To bring them virgins, their plight to mend.

The elders gathered, their minds set free,
They must ensure Benjamin's legacy,
No daughters for them, the vow decree,
Yet an inheritance remained their plea.

A plan was hatched, a feast in Shiloh's land,
Daughters would dance, a chosen band,
From the vineyards of Benjamin, a covert hand,
Would catch them as wives, in the dance so grand.

Fathers and brothers, if they would complain,
Favor they'd seek, for what was gained,
In war they hadn't given, wives' domain,
Their guilt appeased, the plan sustained.

The daughters of Shiloh, caught in the vine,
Became Benjamin's brides, the plan did align,
Their inheritance secured, a tribe's design,
Israel's unity upheld, their fate entwined.

In those days of old, no king's decree,
Each did as right in their own eyes they'd see,
A time of judges, their actions free,
Yet unity struggled, as history would decree.

BITTER RETURN

In days when judges ruled, famine did spread,
Elimelech from Bethlehem fled,
With Naomi his wife, and sons by his side,
To Moab's land, they did confide.

Ephrathites they were, from Judah's kin,
In Moab, their new life did begin,
But Elimelech's life did cease,
Naomi and sons, left in sorrow's lease.

Wives from Moab's daughters they did take,
Orpah and Ruth, bonds did they make,
Ten years passed, then Mahlon and Chilion,
Met death's grasp, Naomi's heart a conundrum.

Alone in a foreign land she stood,
News of bread in Judah's land was good,
With daughters-in-law, her path she chose,
Back to Judah, where her roots arose.

To her daughters-in-law, she advised to part,
To their own kin, she gave her heart,
They wept and clung, reluctant to part,
Orpah turned back, while Ruth chose to start.

Ruth's pledge was strong, steadfast her will,
She'd stay by Naomi, journey uphill,
Where you go, I will go, her vow did stand,
Your people, my people, God of your land.

No death shall part us, Ruth did decree,
Bound by love, where you rest, I will be,
They arrived in Bethlehem, to their delight,
The town stirred, for Naomi, a long-lost sight.

Call me not Naomi, she spoke in pain,
Mara, for bitterness is my name,
Full I went out, now empty I stand,
Almighty's hand, bitter fate in the land.

Ruth, the Moabitess, clung to her side,
From Moab's fields, their journeys did collide,
Barley harvest marked their return's start,
To Bethlehem they came, no longer apart.

HOPE ON THE HORIZON

In the days of old, a kinsman stood,
Boaz, of wealth and kinship's good,
Naomi's husband's family, his name,
He walked in righteousness and fame.

Ruth, the Moabitess, proposed her plea,
"Let me glean, where grace I see,"
Naomi agreed, go, my daughter, go,
To the fields to reap, with the reapers in tow.

In Boaz's field, her steps did light,
Gathering grain till day turned to night,
Kindly Boaz came from Bethlehem town,
"Blessings to you," he spoke with a crown.

To his servant, he queried about the maid,
"Who's this young damsel?" he inquired aid,
A Moabitess, he was informed true,
Returned with Naomi, her fate anew.

Ruth humbly gleaned from morn till eve,
With Boaz's maidens, she'd believe,
He offered protection, kindness to show,
Guiding her way, as the reapers sow.

"Why have I found grace?" Ruth did wonder,
Boaz praised her loyalty like thunder,
He knew her story, the path she had trod,
From Moab's land, to Judah's God.

"May the Lord repay your toil," he said,
A reward for her journey, hardship shed,
Under God's wings, her trust did rest,
In Israel's land, she felt truly blessed.

"Find favor in my sight," Ruth did plead,
Boaz's kindness met her in her need,
At mealtime, he shared bread and vine,
Her hunger quenched, her heart did shine.

He commanded the reapers, "Leave behind,
Handfuls of purpose for Ruth to find,
Glean among sheaves, a bounty embrace,
Reproach her not, let her gather with grace."

She gleaned till evening, the day's labor done,
An ephah of barley she had won,
Into the city, she took her gain,
To Naomi she came, not in vain.

Naomi asked, "Where have you gleaned?"
"Blessed be he who kindness deemed,"
Ruth shared Boaz's name with grace,
Her heart found solace in that place.

Blessed be he of the Lord's great name,
Boaz's kindness to the living and the same,
Near of kin, a next kinsman found,
A glimmer of hope, in life's rebound.

Ruth told Naomi of Boaz's word,
To glean till harvest's end, a promise heard,
Naomi agreed, "Stay with his maidens fair,
In his fields, you shall find care."

Ruth gleaned through barley and wheat's embrace,
Dwelling with Naomi, finding solace and grace,
Their story unfolds with faith intertwined,
In the fields of Boaz, their destinies aligned.

MIDNIGHT ENCOUNTER

Naomi, in counsel, to Ruth did impart,
"Shall I not seek rest for thee, my heart?"
Boaz, our kindred, at the threshing floor,
Winnowing barley, seek him once more.

Wash and anoint, your raiment prepare,
Go to the floor, with cautious care,
Wait till he's done with food and wine,
Then make your move, by plan divine.

Uncover his feet, lie down beside,
Observe his reaction, let time be your guide,
At midnight, he stirred, a woman he'd see,
"Who are you?" he questioned, curiosity free.

"I am Ruth, your handmaid," she declared,
"Spread your skirt over me," she shared,
"Blessed be thou," Boaz replied with grace,
Your kindness shines in this quiet place.

"Fear not, my daughter, I'll fulfill your plea,
A virtuous woman, all the city can see,
Yet there's a kinsman nearer than I,
Stay the night, till morning is nigh.

If he'll do the kinsman's part as he should,
Let him be true, let the matter be good,
But if not, I'll step in, as the Lord lives,
Rest till the morning, the promise it gives."

Ruth lay at his feet till dawn's first light,
She rose, their secret safe from sight,
Boaz gave her barley, vail held in hand,
Into the city, she left the land.

To Naomi, Ruth the tale did unfold,
Of all that happened, the story told,
Six measures of barley, a gift to bear,
Boaz's kindness beyond compare.

Naomi advised, "Wait and see,
How the matter unfolds, what will be,
Rest assured, he'll act without delay,
Until this matter is settled today."

SEALED WITH A SHOE

Boaz, to the gate, made his way,
The kinsman he sought, without delay,
"Turn aside, sit down," he cried out loud,
With elders of the city, forming a crowd.

Naomi's land for sale, he conveyed,
Elimelech's portion, he displayed,
"I thought to let you know," he began,
You have the chance, as next of kin.

"If you'll redeem it, declare your intent,
For none else has the right, I am content,
But if not, speak now," Boaz did say,
The kinsman replied, "I will redeem today."

Then Boaz revealed the fuller scope,
"Ruth, the Moabitess, part of the hope,
The wife of the dead, you must take as well,
To raise his name, his legacy to tell."

But the kinsman declined with due care,
Lest his inheritance be impaired, unfair,
He passed on the chance, left it for Boaz,
The custom of that time, then followed as was.

The shoe was removed, the deal was sealed,
A testimony sure, in custom revealed,
Boaz bought the land, and more than that too,
Ruth, the Moabitess, his wife, so true.

Before all witnesses, their vows were heard,
Their covenant sealed, every word,
A child they conceived, by the Lord's grace,
Obed was born, a cherished embrace.

Naomi rejoiced, for a kinsman she gained,
Her life restored, as blessings rained,
Obed, the restorer, the name so sweet,
A nourisher of age, a life complete.

Naomi cradled the child, her heart stirred,
The women nearby, the news they heard,
Obed's name they gave with joy and acclaim,
The lineage of David, a part of his name.

Generations passed, the line did unfold,
Pharez, Hezron, their stories told,
Ram, Amminadab, Nahshon, and more,
Boaz, Obed, Jesse, David they bore.

COVENANT KEEPERS

Also in the
Threads of Revelation Series:

Pillar of Fire:
Toward the Promised Land

Dawn of Eternity
Edens Legacy Unravelled

Destiny's Dance:
Footprints In The Wilderness

Hi. I hope you have enjoyed this book. If you have a moment to spare, I would greatly appreciate it if you could take the time to review it.

If you gained valuable insights, or if your spiritual journey was influenced in any way, I would love to hear about it. Your opinion matters to me and I would be grateful if you could share your experience and thoughts by leaving a review.

www.ingramcontent.com/pod-product-compliance
Lightning Source LLC
Chambersburg PA
CBHW060837050426
42453CB00008B/731